First Facts®

EXTREME PLANET

# THE COLDEST PLACES ON EARTH

by Jennifer M. Besel

**Consultant:**
Randall S. Cerveny, PhD
President's Professor, School of Geographical Sciences
Arizona State University, Tempe

CAPSTONE PRESS
a capstone imprint

First Facts is published by Capstone Press,
151 Good Counsel Drive, P.O. Box 669, Mankato, Minnesota 56002.
www.capstonepress.com

092009
005618CGS10

 Books published by Capstone Press are manufactured with paper
containing at least 10 percent post-consumer waste.

*Library of Congress Cataloging-in-Publication Data*
Besel, Jennifer M.
    The coldest places on Earth / by Jennifer M. Besel.
    p. cm. — (First facts. Extreme planet)
    Summary: "An introduction to the coldest places on Earth, including maps and colorful
photographs" — Provided by publisher.
    Includes bibliographical references and index.
    ISBN 978-1-4296-3961-3 (library binding)
    1. Climatic extremes — Juvenile literature. 2. Arctic regions — Description and travel — Juvenile
literature.  I. Title. II. Series.
QC981.8.C53B474 2010
910.911 — dc22                                                    2009026031

**Editorial credits**
Erika L. Shores, editor; Ted Williams, designer; Svetlana Zhurkin, media researcher;
    Eric Manske, production specialist

**Photo credits**
Corbis/Arctic-Images, 9; Visuals Unlimited, 7
Digital Vision, 5
Getty Images/National Geographic/Gordon Wiltsie, 21; The Image Bank/Daisy Gilardini,
10; National Geographic/Maria Stenzel, 19; Taxi/Howard Platt, cover;
iStockphoto/Richard Gunion, 13; Viktor Zimbachevskij, 15
Ned Rozell, 16

Essential content terms are **bold** and are defined at the bottom of the spread
where they first appear.

# TABLE OF CONTENTS

# THE EARTH'S FREEZER

 Imagine living in a place as cold as your freezer. Do you think it's possible? Well, people and animals deal with extreme cold all over the planet.

 The sun heats the earth. But some places don't get enough sunshine to warm up. Other spots have a high **elevation**, which keeps them quite cold. Let's visit seven of these chilly places.

> **elevation** — the height above sea level; sea level is defined as zero elevation.

# 7 DEEP SEA

Almost no sunlight reaches the ocean floor. Down there, the water is always about 34° F (1° C). That temperature might not seem very cold. But compare it to a swimming pool. Most pools are 80° F (27° C).

**EXTREME FACT!**

The deep sea covers about 67 percent of earth. Squid, fish, and other ocean animals live in this cold place.

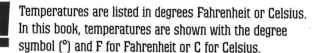

Temperatures are listed in degrees Fahrenheit or Celsius. In this book, temperatures are shown with the degree symbol (°) and F for Fahrenheit or C for Celsius.

□ **DEEP SEA**

• Squid are suited for life in the cold water of the deep sea.

# 6 ICEHOTEL

During winter in **Jukkasjärvi**, Sweden, visitors stay in a hotel made of ice. Guests sleep on ice blocks. Reindeer hides and sleeping bags keep the chill away. If you visit, bring your slippers. The temperature in the ICEHOTEL is only 23° F (-5° C).

Jukkasjärvi: YOU-cahs-yahr-vee

Jukkasjärvi, Sweden

NORTH POLE

EXTREME FACT!

July is the North Pole's warmest month. But the temperatures only reach about 32° F (0° C).

# COLD!

# NORTH POLE

The top of the earth is icy cold. During winter, the North Pole is tipped away from the sun. Sunlight can't reach the pole to heat it up. Temperatures drop way below **freezing**.

> **freezing** — the temperature at which water becomes a solid; water freezes at 32° F (0° C).

# 4 MOUNT MCKINLEY

Mount McKinley is the highest mountain in North America. Temperatures at its **peak** drop to -40° F (-40° C). Winds blow up to 100 miles (161 kilometers) per hour. With the **windchill**, the temperature feels like -100° F (-73° C).

**peak** — the top of a mountain
**windchill** — a measurement that reports the combined effect of low temperature and wind speed

MOUNT MCKINLEY

N
W E
S

# 3 YAKUTSK, RUSSIA

**Yakutsk**, in eastern Russia, is the coldest city in the world. More than 200,000 people live there. In January, the highest temperature is only -40° F (-40° C). People don't wear metal eyeglasses outside during the winter. The metal could freeze to their faces.

> Yakutsk: yah-KUTSK

Want a snow day in Yakutsk? You'll have to hope the temperature drops below -67° F (-55° C).

**EXTREME FACT!**

14

YAKUTSK, RUSSIA

SNAG, YUKON TERRITORY

EXTREME FACT!

In 2003, Jim Brader from the National Weather Service visited Snag. He braved the cold to learn more about the record-setting day in 1947.

# SNAG, YUKON TERRITORY

Snag is a tiny town in western Canada. On February 3, 1947, the temperature in Snag was -81° F (-63° C). That temperature was a record. In North America, no other place has ever been that cold.

# 1 ANTARCTICA

Antarctica is the world's coldest place. For six months a year, the **continent** is dark and very, very cold. Powerful winds swirl across the icy ground. At the South Pole in Antarctica, temperatures never rise above freezing.

> **continent** — one of earth's seven large land masses

ANTARCTICA

N
W · E
S

Antarctica holds the record for the lowest air temperature on earth. On July 21, 1983, the temperature dropped to -128.5° F (-89° C).

Antarctica is just one of earth's cold places. All around the world, people and animals live in chilly places. That's pretty cool!

**EXTREME FACT!**

Penguins and seals live on Antarctica's coasts. But no animals live in the center of Antarctica. It's too cold there.

# GLOSSARY

**continent** (KAHN-tuh-nuhnt) — one of earth's seven large land masses

**elevation** (el-uh-VAY-shuhn) — the height above sea level; sea level is defined as zero elevation.

**freezing** (FREEZ-ing) — the temperature at which water becomes a solid; water freezes at 32° F (0° C).

**peak** (PEEK) — the pointed top of a mountain

**pole** (POHL) — the top or bottom part of a planet

**windchill** (WIND-chil) — a measurement given in degrees that reports the effect of low temperature and wind speed on the human body

# READ MORE

**Adil, Janeen R.** *Why Is the South Pole so Cold?: A Book about Antarctica.* Why in the World? Mankato, Minn.: Capstone Press, 2007.

**Gill, Shelley.** *Up on Denali: Alaska's Wild Mountain.* Seattle: Sasquatch Books, 2006.

**Hyde, Natalie.** *Deep Sea Extremes.* Extreme Nature. New York: Crabtree, 2009.

# INTERNET SITES

FactHound offers a safe, fun way to find Internet sites related to this book. All of the sites on FactHound have been researched by our staff.

Here's all you do:

Visit *www.facthound.com*

FactHound will fetch the best sites for you!

# INDEX